FROM RIVETS AND RAILS

Recipes of a Railroad
Boarding House Cookbook

SHAUNDA KENNEDY WENGER

Based upon the early 1900s cookery journal
of Elizabeth Shade Kennedy

Essemkay Company Productions

Copyright © 2012 Shaunda Kennedy Wenger

All rights reserved.

ISBN: 0615730426
ISBN-13: 978-0615730424

DEDICATION

To Mom & Dad,
because my love for food and family
is rooted in your kitchen

and

To my grandmother, Martha Grugan Kennedy,
who gave me a treasure
found in a cookery journal

NYC & Hudson River Railroad Shops
Avis, PA

CONTENTS

	Foreword	i
1	Beverages	1
2	Meat Cure	7
3	Fruit Butters & Preserves	9
4	Sauces, Dressings, & Pickles	15
5	Main Dishes & Sides	28
6	Desserts	38
7	Cookies & Treats	55
8	Medicinals & Miscellanies	67

FOREWORD

Notes about Avis and the NYC Railroad Shops

Prior to the arrival of the railroad repair shops that began servicing the New York Central and Hudson River Railroad after 1901, Avis, Pennsylvania, was a small, rural town named Oak Grove. With no "improved" roads, Oak Grove had only two main connections with the outside world: the first, as a minor stop for the stagecoach line, and the second, as a minor stop for the West Branch Canal which was used for transportation along the Susquehanna River. However, the rural and isolated lifestyle of Oak Grove soon changed (along with its name) after the railroad shops were built. In a few short years, Avis grew into an industrial boomtown with over 1,000 skilled mechanics working in the shops alone, and by 1910 Charles William Kennedy, who had previously worked at the shops and roundhouse in nearby Altoona, sat at the shop's helm as superintendent.

How were all these workers accommodated? Some, of course, moved into the area, fueling the local housing market. Others commuted, many by rail, to their stations of employment.

From the beginning of railroading and up through the early 1900s, it was common for railroad employees and mechanics to ride the rails for their "run of work" or out to the shops and roundhouses that were located along the tracks, where they would stay for a week or two, collect their wages, and then return home for a short leave to reconnect with family. These workers counted on the hospitality of "boarding houses" to be their home-away-from-home in providing a temporary place to hang their hat. Elizabeth Shade Kennedy provided one of these such respites, and with the death of her husband in 1920, this livelihood became a means of survival for herself and her family.

Elizabeth's boarding house, which made use of the spare rooms in her home, not only provided workers and travelers with a place to stay, but also a place to eat. Many found a meal at her table. It is reported that she served meals three times a day for up to 15 people. With so many to cook for and so much responsibility in providing for her five sons as a single mother, it is not surprising that she kept a cookery journal while doing so. This cookbook is based on that journal.

Thoughts About Elizabeth

Elizabeth Shade Kennedy lived through a period of American history that was wrought with unimaginable hardship and incredible accomplishment brought on by a generation that nearly lost everything and found the grit and determination to rise from it all. She was part of the generation that moved from a dependence on horses to engine-driven machinery. She was part of the generation that survived the Great Depression and went on to further define technological advancements in the agricultural revolution, the industrial revolution, and the expansion of the American railroads. She was part of a generation that lived through the first World War and then faced the Second. She was part of a generation that survived the Spanish flu epidemic of 1918 and then went on to develop vaccines to combat the next: polio. And lastly, through it all, she was part of a generation that didn't escape the pain and suffering of loss. As a young woman, she endured the loss of three daughters and her husband.

If the framework around which Elizabeth's life was built left her with the means and knowledge to get by, it was her determination to properly raise her five boys as a single parent that was the hub around which her wheels turned. The country was opening up around them, and she helped put them on a road to success. The industry which had provided her husband with a career became a cornerstone from which she would carve out her own livelihood.

Thoughts on the Cookbook

One can only imagine the blow Elizabeth took with the unexpected death of her husband in 1920. Judging from the care Elizabeth took in recording her recipes, the notes on preparation, and suggestions on the presentation of food, it appears she put a tremendous amount of work into providing for her family and guests. The recipes presented here depict a time during which modern conveniences were just beginning to arise. Although homes were slowly improving with the addition of appliances such as the radio and refrigerator, most families were still largely dependent on stocking their own shelves. And for those who had a steady influx of guests, the need to keep pantries supplied weighed even larger.

This cookbook is somewhat of a testament to the foundation that modern methods of food preservation and procurement were built upon. It also offers insight into the foundations from which some of our more fanciful recipes, (such as your fruit mango salsas) may have emerged through misinterpretation of historic recipes. Lastly, it offers a window into the possibilities that are inherent in the kitchen—possibilities that may become lost in a society that is increasingly dependent on *modern convenience.*

It is my hope that this cookbook will offer a jumping point from which to sit back and contemplate what it truly means to be self-sufficient, and perhaps more importantly, explore one simple yet limitless question: *What if?*

1 BEVERAGES

Rose Blossom Wine

1 qt blossoms
4 lbs sugar
3 qts boiling water

1 lemon sliced thin
white of one egg
3 Tbsp yeast

  Place blossoms and sugar in water and bring to a boil. Stir until sugar is dissolved. Remove from heat and let stand until cool. Then add the slices of lemon, egg white, and yeast. Let this mixture stand for another 24 hours. Strain and bottle, but do not cork until yeast is done working.

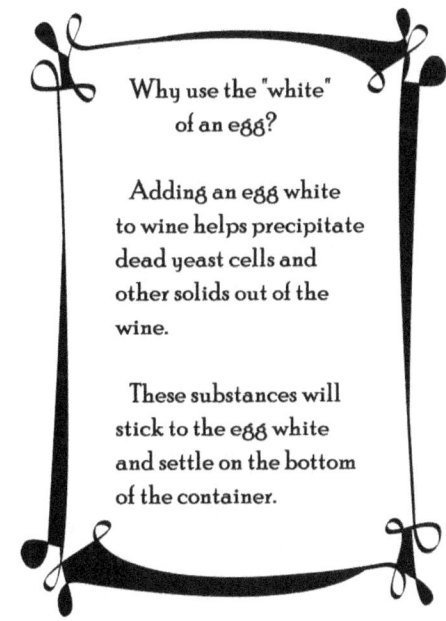

Why use the "white" of an egg?

Adding an egg white to wine helps precipitate dead yeast cells and other solids out of the wine.

These substances will stick to the egg white and settle on the bottom of the container.

Elder Blossom Wine

2 qts elder blossoms
1 gallon of water
5 lbs white sugar

1 lemon, sliced thin
white of one egg
1 Tbsp hop yeast

Bring the water to a boil. Stir in sugar until it is dissolved. Pour the hot sugar-water on top of the blossoms and let cool. When the blossom mixture is room temperature, add lemon slices, and yeast. Let it ferment for three days in a vessel covered with a blanket, then strain through a cheesecloth and add the white of an egg, beaten lightly.

> **What is hop yeast?**
> Hop yeast refers to dry yeast cakes made from hop blossoms.
> Lupulin oil from hop blossoms was valued for its preservative properties in making beer, while hops were valued as a leavening agent in making bread.
> Hop yeast cakes were a kitchen staple until the late 1800s when commercial yeast became more available.

Dandelion Wine

1 qt dandelions
3 qts boiling water
4 lbs sugar
2 lemons, or more
1 Tbsp of yeast
white of one egg

Bring the water to a boil. Stir in sugar until it is dissolved. Pour the hot sugar-water on top of the dandelions and let cool. After it has cooled, add yeast and 2 sliced lemons for every gallon of liquid. Let this mixture ferment 10 or 12 days, then strain. Add egg white to settle solids from the liquid. Let the mixture stand for a while, then skim, and put away.

Don't cork up tight, or bottles will burst!

a note on prohibition

Since early colonial days many groups, such as The Women's Christian Temperance Union, believed that consumption of liquor created poor social norms and unruly behavior resulting in higher incidences of crime and spousal abuse. The drive for prohibition was further fueled in WWI when government mandated that all grain would go to the war effort and none would be used for alcohol production.

However, The Volsted Act which enacted prohibition didn't become law until after the war ended.

Curiously, wine-making for personal use was not out-lawed, because wine was considered to be a "non-intoxicating" drink.

Red Sour Cherry Wine

1 qt cherry juice
3 qts water
3 qts sugar
yeast

Put the ingredients into a suitable vessel (non-metal) and let them ferment. Skim every morning until no scum comes up. Then put the wine in a keg or jug, leaving cork partly open. Keep filling up until the yeast is done working, then bottle.

If the fruit is mashed, put the cherries in the vessel with the juice. Let the cherries remain for 2 or 3 days, then take the cherries out and heat (not boil) so as to draw the red out of them. Return this liquid to the wine vessel and discard mash and pits.

Obviously, experienced wine makers will know what to do with the instructions in Elizabeth Shade Kennedy's journal, while beginners will want to consult modern wine-making guides.

Blackberry Cordial

berries (enough to render a pint of juice)
1 pt sugar
1 oz cinnamon
¼ oz ground mace
2 tsp ground cloves
1 pt brandy

    Wash berries and put them in a pot on the stove. Heat them over low to medium heat in order to draw the juice out of them. Strain the berries, saving the juice and discarding the seeds and mash. Combine one pint of the juice with sugar, cinnamon, mace and cloves and heat slowly for fifteen minutes. Let mixture cool completely, then add one pint of brandy. Strain and bottle.

"Mr. Ready coming"

Rhubarb Wine

1 qt rhubarb
1 lemon
1 orange
4 qts water
3 lbs sugar
½ yeast cake

    Grind the fruits together in a food chopper. Dissolve the sugar in boiling water. Place the fruit in a large vessel and cover with the sugar-water. Let stand overnight. Then add the yeast cake and let the mixture stand for another 3 or 4 days. Strain the mixture through a cloth and bottle, but don't cork yet! You can put a couple of raisins in each bottle if you wish. Let the bottles stand for about 3 weeks before you cork.

We love this note at the top of the recipe! It shows anticipation of an upcoming visit and efforts made to plan a special menu, which included rhubarb wine. However, the question remains… Who was Mr. Ready?

Bennett Beer

3 tsp salt
2 lbs sugar
1 can Blue Ribbon Light Malt
1 cake Fleishman yeast

Put a big dishpan of hot water on stove. Warm the can of Blue Ribbon Malt flavoring in a tea kettle of hot water. Mix the salt, sugar, and malt into the hot water and stir until dissolved. Let cool until lukewarm. Add the yeast. Pour the mixture into a 5 gallon crock and fill to top with cold water. Let stand and ferment.

There is nothing like a cook who is determined to please the guests at her table. However, what would serious "home brewers" think about the use of a "tea kettle" in the production of beer?!

Cocoa

The progressive housewife should have a bottle or jar of cocoa syrup on hand, then it takes only a few minutes to have a cup of hot cocoa; or one can have a glass of iced cocoa when tired or fatiqued; or heated and thickened, and you have a sauce for ice cream.

Material to make a jar of syrup ~ one cup cocoa, 2 cups sugar, 2 cups water, 1/2 teaspoon salt.
Utensils ~ saucepan, measuring cup, teaspoon, small bowl.

How to make ~ put the water and sugar in saucepan, stir until dissolved, put on a fire and boil for 5 minutes; mix cocoa with cold water to make a paste and add to boiling water and sugar; boil slowly for 10 minutes; add salt. When cold put in bottles or glass jar and store in the refrigerator and you are prepared for any emergency.

*One of a few newspaper clippings saved in the journal. The **Avis Advance** was published on Fridays. Subscriptions were $1 a year paid in advance, or $1.25 otherwise.*

Hershey Chocolate Syrup wasn't available until 1926. Bosco Chocolate Syrup followed in 1928 from New Jersey.

FROM RIVETS AND RAILS

Local businesses operating in Avis in the early 1900s

The Bonner House, a popular hotel and restaurant
Telegraph exchange
The *Avis Advance* newspaper
The Seyler sisters' millinery shop
David Schaffer's jewelry store
Corning Glass
Oak Grove Bottling Works
J.T. McGuire's "Pioneer Store"
D.P. Dorman's grocery store
Bonner's grocery store
Love's Hardware
Reichard's Bakery
Leo Earon's meat market
John Brungard's meat market
Edward Meyers's meat market
Oak Grove Pharmacy
Schaffer's Drug Store
Martin May's Barber Shop
The Buffalo Clothing House
Mayrun's Candy Store
Mansurry's Dentistry
R.H. Meek's Medical Practice
Schroeder's Barber Shop
A glove factory
A livery
J.T. Brickly, coal distributor
Getz and Sweeley, building contractors

The NYC Railroad line repair shops

"Kettle" was another term for locomotive.

2 MEAT CURE

This recipe gets a chapter of its own: curing instructions for large quantities of meat.

The salting and smoking of meat for preservation has been practiced since before the birth of Christ, with references dated as far back as the time of Homer. The application of a salt brine prevents contamination and deterioration by bacteria, while smoking adds flavor and tenderization. It is known that Native American tribes smoked their meat by hanging it at the top of their teepees above their campfires. Europeans and American settlers typically used a separate building called a smokehouse, where meats were smoked for two weeks or more and then stored.

The most commonly cured cuts of pork include the ham, shoulders, belly, loin, and jowl. Cuts of cured beef include the briskets, strips of round or chuck, and plates which are cured as strips of beef bacon.

Mrs. Kennedy's Meat Cure

For 1000 lbs of pork, take 12 quarts of salt, 3 lbs of good brown sugar, and 1 lb of pepper.

Mix these three ingredients in gradually together, then take another pound of salt and dissolve it in 1 quart of boiling water and pour it over the dry mixture above and mix again.

Then rub the meat with the mixture, and let lay for 8 or 10 days, going over the meat three different times throughout this period.

Then hang your meat and smoke.

> Given the need for cold temperatures during the curing and smoking processes, hogs and other livestock traditionally were slaughtered at the onset of winter.
>
> Salt is the primary ingredient for curing. It prevents bacterial growth by dehydration. It also adds flavor.

This recipe came from Elizabeth's mother-in-law, Catherine Hayes Kennedy.

The kitchen car was the caboose.

3 FRUIT BUTTERS & PRESERVES

Quince Honey

3 apples (peeled, cored, chopped)
3 quinces (grated)
3 lbs sugar
1 qt water

Boil the sugar and water together for 10 minutes, then add quinces and apples and cook another 25 minutes. Put into clean glass jars and seal.

Grape Butter

1 qt grapes
4 cups sugar
4 Tbsp water

Put all ingredients in a pan and bring to a boil. Continue to boil for 10 to 15 minutes, and stir while doing so. Put the mixture through a sieve and into sterilized jars, and seal.

Apple Butter

8 cups apples (peeled, cored, chopped)
2 tsp cinnamon
1 tsp cloves
1 tsp nutmeg
½ tsp salt
6 cups of dark brown sugar
2 cups of cider

Mix all ingredients in a pan and bring to a gentle boil. Stir frequently until butter becomes thick. This will take about one hour. Pour into sterilized jars and seal.

> Fruit butters are a fruit puree made from cooked fruit that is put through a strainer to get a fine pulp without a lot of juice.
>
> Unlike jams and jellies, fruit butters do not require pectin, but only use sugar and stirring over heat to prevent burning.

Ginger Pears

9 lbs pears
6 lbs sugar
4 cups water
4 lemons
6 oz crystallized ginger

Pare fruit and cut into thin slices, removing core. Drop the fruit into a weak salt-water solution to prevent discoloring. Drain from salt water and add to boiling syrup made with sugar and water. Simmer until the fruit begins to look clear around the edges and add the grated rind of 2 lemons and juice of all four. Add ginger cut in tiny bits and simmer until mixture is thick and pears are transparent. Put into sterilized jelly jars and cover with a thin layer of paraffin. When cold, cover with more paraffin. Store in a dark, cool place.

A "Jam buster" was the assistant yardmaster.

Spiced Pears

6 lbs pears
5 cups light brown sugar
2 cups cider vinegar
¼ cup broken cinnamon and whole cloves, mixed.

Pare, halve and core pears before weighing. Place in a crock, alternating with layers of sugar. Pour vinegar over the top of the layers and let stand overnight.

Drain the liquid into a separate container and add the spices tied in a cheesecloth bag. Bring this mixture to a boil and boil five minutes. Add the pears and simmer until tender but not broken or soft. Pack in hot sterilized jars and cover with boiling syrup. Seal at once.

If the vinegar is very sharp, it should be diluted with water.

Peach and Pineapple Conserves

2 cups diced peaches
1 cup of cooked diced pineapple or grated pineapple
Juice and grated rind of 1 orange
Juice and grated rind of 1 lemon
2 2/3 cups of sugar

Combine all ingredients in a pan and cook over low heat until thick and clear. Stir frequently to prevent scorching. Put into sterile hot glasses and seal immediately with paraffin.

> Paraffin is a wax that was commonly used in canning jams and jellies. A layer of the melted wax was poured over the top of jellies to seal out air and inhibit growth of bacteria.
>
> Paraffin also gives a shiny quality to chocolates, when added.

Canned Pineapple

Pare the pineapple, taking out the "eyes." Tear the pineapple into pieces with a silver fork. For every pound of pineapple, you will need ¾ lb of sugar. Put the pineapple into a porcelain kettle, add the sugar, and cook over a very moderate fire for ten minutes. Put into jars and seal.

Canned Raspberries or Strawberries

Select as many firm berries as you wish to preserve. After washing them, place them in heated jars, filling them to the rim. Cover the berries with a boiling syrup made of equal parts sugar and water. Cover the jars with lids and place them in a tub or other receptacle deep enough to hold water to cover them. Pour boiling water into the tub until jars are submerged and let the jars stand in the water until it is cold. Fruit will be found to be perfectly cooked. Berries, canned in this way, retain color, shape, and fresh flavor.

Spiced Crabapples

Crabapples (as much as you would like to preserve)
8 cups water
6 cups sugar
1 tsp ground cloves
1 tsp cinnamon

Place spices in a cheesecloth bag and suspend in the sugar-water syrup (made by boiling sugar and water previously). Bring this to a boil again and add crabapples. Keep the crabapples on medium heat until the skins crack. Remove the crabapples. Peel, core, and halve. Pack in clean jars and cover with more syrup. Add some whole cloves and cinnamon to the jars and seal while hot.

My great maternal grandmother also preserved crabapples in the fall. They were delicious, served warm with a pork roast or ham, or cold as a condiment.

Sweet Pickled Pears

4 cups sugar
2 cups vinegar (not too sharp)
3 dozen pears, small and firm
whole cloves
cinnamon sticks

Cut out the blossom end (bottom) of fruit and pierce it several times with fork. Push a whole clove into the blossom end of each pear. Make a syrup of sugar and vinegar in a large pot, and after it has boiled 5 minutes drop in as many pears as possible without crowding each other. Cook gently over medium heat until pears are tender. Remove pears, place them in clean, hot jars and cover them with syrup. Put a piece of cinnamon in each jar, cover, and seal.

Tomato Mincemeat

1 peck green tomatoes
5 lbs of brown sugar,
2 lbs raisins
1 cup vinegar
2 Tbsp cinnamon
1 Tbsp allspice
1 Tbsp cloves
2 Tbsp salt
6 large tart apples (cored, peeled and chopped fine)

Core and grind the tomatoes. Drain the juice and add the sugar and raisins. Cook over medium heat until tomatoes are tender. Add the vinegar and spices, and boil until thickened. Add the apples, and continue cooking over heat until the apples are tender. Put mincemeat into clean jars and seal while hot.

> **What is a peck?**
>
> A peck is a measurement that was historically used at produce farms. It is equal to 8 quarts, or 13.25 pounds, or 1/4 of a bushel. In this kitchen, 18 baseball-sized tomatoes would have amounted to one peck.

When making pies, add a little butter.

Mrs. Kennedy's Mincemeat

2 lbs beef, chopped fine
2 lbs beef suet (firm beef fat)
2 lbs currants
2 lbs raisins
1 lb citron
1 ½ lb canned lemon peel
4 lbs apples (peeled, cored, chopped)
2 lbs sugar
2 nutmegs, grated
¼ oz cloves
½ oz cinnamon
¼ oz mace
1 tsp salt
2 lemons, juice & grated rind
2 oranges, juice & grated rind

Place all ingredients in a large pan and simmer over medium-low heat for about 2 hours. Pack into clean hot jars and seal. Add brandy when making pies, if desired.

This recipe was from Elizabeth's mother-in-law, Catherine Hayes Kennedy.

a note on mincemeat

Mincemeat was developed as a way of preserving meat about 500 years ago in England. Although it is commonly found on tables as a dessert pie, traditionally, it began as a main meal, stuffed with more meat than fruit.

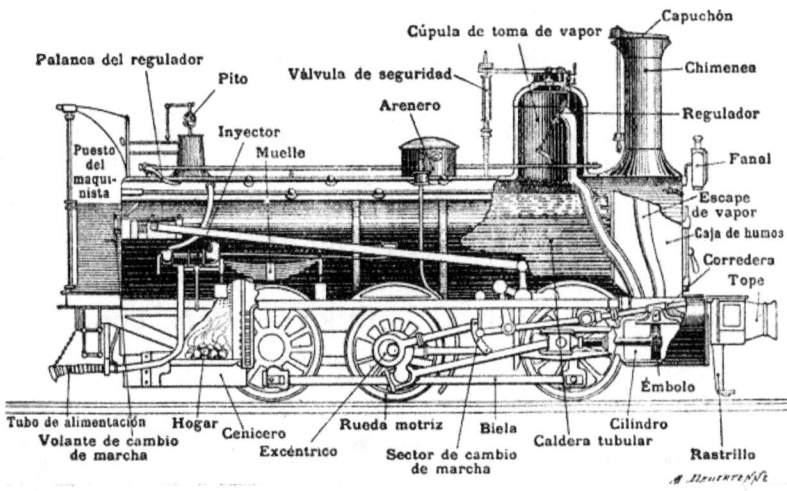

4 SAUCES, DRESSINGS & PICKLES

Cold Ketchup

½ peck* ripe tomatoes (cored, seeded, chopped fine)
1 cup onions (chopped fine)
1 cup horseradish
2 red peppers (seeded, chopped fine)
3 stalks celery (chopped very fine)
1 cup whole mustard seed
½ cup salt
1 Tbsp black pepper
½ cup sugar
1 qt vinegar
you can add celery seeds (chopped fine, optional)

What is a peck? see Tomato Mincemeat recipe on page 13

Put all ingredients in a pan and cook over medium heat until tender. Place in a grinder. Then put through a fine sieve, and seal in jars.

Mango Sandwich Spread

18 mangos (seeds removed). Scald these in boiling water, then let stand until cold. Put mangos through a grinder. Add salt, vinegar, and sugar, to taste, but don't let the spread become too runny. Bring this mixture to a boil. Put in 1 jar of French Mustard, if desired. Thicken the mixture with a batter of flour paste (made with a little bit of water). Stir in 3 stalks of celery, chopped very fine.

> ### What were mangos?
>
> Today we know a mango as a fruit, but use of the word "mango" for bell peppers is believed to have originated with the coal mining communities of Pennsylvania. In the 1887 edition of "The Original White House Cook Book," a recipe for Green Pepper Mangos describes the bell pepper perfectly in removing the seeds and filling it with a vegetable mixture.

Table Mustard

Put 3 teaspoons of mustard in a bowl. Pour just enough warm water to make a stiff paste. Rub until smooth, then add ¼ cup vinegar, 1 tablespoon sugar, a pinch salt, and ½ teaspoon cornstarch. Then add then beaten yolks of two eggs. Set this mixture in a double boiler and stir until the mixture thickens. Add a lump of butter, about size of an egg.

Mayonnaise Dressing

1 tsp mustard
1 tsp salt
1 tsp powdered sugar
½ tsp paprika, or dash of cayenne pepper
yolks of 2 eggs
2 Tbsp lemon juice
2 Tbsp vinegar
1 ½ cup oil

Add egg yolks to dry ingredients and mix well. Add 1 ½ teaspoons of vinegar, then add oil drop-by-drop at first and stir constantly. As dressing thickens, thin with vinegar or lemon juice until all the liquid is used. If oil is added too rapidly, the dressing will look curdled. Should this occur, slowly add the yolk of another egg to restore to smoothness. The oil should be cold, and it works well to set the bowl you are working with in a larger one containing *cracked ice* while mixing the dressing.

A teaspoon of peanut butter thoroughly mixed into the mayonnaise adds to the flavor.

a note on ice
cracked, chipped, and cubed

Before refrigeration, food was kept cold in ice boxes that were stocked with 100-pound blocks of ice.

When ice was desired for cooling a beverage, for example, ice picks were used to chip pieces off the blocks.

In 1928 the first ice cube tray was invented by Lloyd Copeman, after he noticed snow slipping off his rubber boots as he collected maple sap in the woods. After a few experiments, he came up with the rubber ice cube tray. The steel tray followed in 1933 with the design by Guy Tinkham.

Salad Dressing

4 egg yolks
½ cup sugar
1 tsp salt
3 Tbsp flour

½ tsp paprika
2-3 cups vinegar
½ cup water
2 Tbsp butter

Beat yolks, add dry ingredients and mix well. Add the remaining ingredients and cook in a double boiler over medium heat. Stir frequently. The dressing is done when it is thick and creamy. Mix well, cool and chill. If dressing is too thick when ready to use, thin it with sweet or sour cream.

Dressing

Mix 1 cup flour with 6 tablespoons mustard, 1 tablespoon turmeric, and 5 cups sugar (or to taste). Add these dry ingredients to 1 quart of water and 1 quart of vinegar (diluted). Stir all together and cook over medium heat for 10 minutes. Then add 1 ounce of celery seed and 1 cup mustard seed. Seal in jars while hot.

French Dressing

2 Tbsp vinegar
4 Tbsp Olive Oil

½ tsp salt
½ tsp pepper

Add the seasonings to oil, then add vinegar and stir until well blended.

An "icing charge" was a fee for keeping perishable freight on ice.

French Dressing

1 Tbsp vinegar
3 Tbsp olive oil
1 tsp salt

1 tsp pepper
a little scraped onion

Hard Sauce

½ cup butter (melted)
1 cup sugar (pulverized)
dash of nutmeg

½ tsp vanilla
whites of one egg (beaten very stiff)

Combine the first four ingredients and mix well. Gently stir in the egg white and then add your brandy.

Bordeaux Sauce

2 gallons cabbage (chopped fine)
1 gallon green tomatoes (cored, seeds removed, and chopped fine)
1 dozen onions (chopped fine)
1 gallon vinegar
¼ lb white mustard seed
1 oz allspice

1 oz turmeric
1 qt celery (chopped fine)
1 oz ginger
1 oz pepper
1 oz cloves
1 ¼ lbs sugar
1 ¾ lbs salt
1 doz sweet green peppers

Mix all the ingredients together, bring to a boil, and simmer for 20 minutes. Seal in small glass jars.

This is very nice with all kinds of meat or fish.

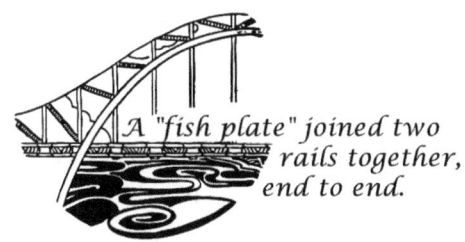

A "fish plate" joined two rails together, end to end.

Chili Sauce

36 large ripe tomatoes (1 peck)
6 onions
4 peppers (seeds removed)
8 cups vinegar
1 ½ cups sugar
2 Tbsp salt
3 tsp red pepper
2 tsp cloves
2 tsp cinnamon
2 tsp allspice
2 tsp ginger
1 tsp nutmeg

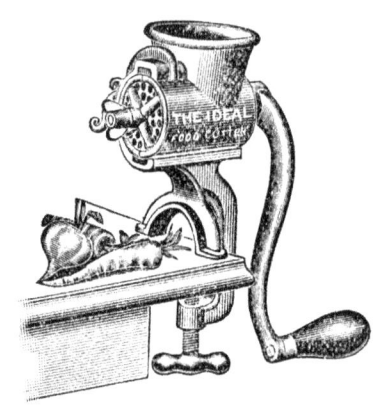

Chop onions and peppers together. Put tomatoes through a meat grinder, then simmer all ingredients together until dark.

The Universal meat grinder was designed in 1897. It improved the life of every kitchen cook that gained access to one, with its ability to grind two pounds of meat in a minute. Versatile cooks quickly caught on to the idea that it could be used to grind fruits and vegetables, as well.

Chili Sauce ~ A.P.C.

4 onions (chopped)
2 green peppers (seeds removed and chopped)
2 Tbsp salt
1 Tbsp cloves
2 grated nutmegs
2 tsp cinnamon
½ cup sugar
1 cup vinegar
12 ripe tomatoes

Combine the tomatoes, onions, and salt and simmer for two hours. Add the sugar and vinegar and simmer another 30 minutes. Add the spices and peppers and simmer a few more minutes. Jar and seal.

Wine Sauce

Put ¼ cup of butter, ¼ cup of sugar, 1 beaten egg, 1 cup boiling water, and 1 glass of white wine or brandy into a pan and let simmer for 10 minutes.

Pepper Relish

18 mangos (red, yellow, green bell peppers, seeds removed)
16 medium-sized onions (chopped fine)
3 stalks celery (chopped fine)
½ lb sugar
1 ½ qts cider vinegar

Grind mangos first and then salt accordingly to taste. Pour boiling water over peppers and let stand for ½ hour; then drain and mix in onions, salt, sugar, and celery. Add the cider vinegar and simmer for ¾ hour. Seal in clean jars.

Barrie Barnes India Relish

2 qts green tomatoes (chopped fine)
1 qt white onions (chopped fine)
1 head cabbage or cauliflower (chopped fine)
3 red or green mangos (bell peppers, seeds removed, chopped fine)
1 stalk celery (chopped fine)
1 cup salt in 4 qt water

Combine all ingredients and let stand overnight. Drain and scald in hot water for 3 minutes, and then drain again.

We believe you will want to add vinegar to this recipe, as was done for the pepper relish.

Green Tomato Soy

1 gallon green tomatoes	Salt
1 pint of onions, or more	Vinegar

Place the tomatoes and onions in a kettle in alternating layers of salt. Let stand awhile, and then drain. Put in a kettle on the stove, cover with vinegar, and simmer until done.

Barrie Smith's Green Tomato Chow

1 dozen mangos (bell peppers)	5 carrots
10 onions	Salt
½ peck tomatoes	Sugar
4 stalks of celery	Turmeric
1 head of cauliflower	Cinnamon

Chop tomatoes, removing seeds, and then put through a grinder with carrots and cauliflower. Cover with water and a little salt and cook for 5 minutes. Drain these in a colander and let them set for an hour. Return them to the kettle and add celery that has been chopped fine and onions that have been put through a grinder. Add salt, sugar, and spices to taste. Mix all together, then put in a bag and drain overnight. Return to kettle, bringing to a boil, then put in bottles and seal.

a note on canning

Traditional canning methods are used to destroy harmful microorganisms by eliminating germs in the jar through boiling and pushing out air from the jar through processing. Two common methods for canning are pressure-canning and water-boiling. Water-boiling is fine for high-acid foods like tomatoes, pickles, and jams. Pressure-canning is used for low-acid foods like meat and fish.

Mrs. King's Bread & Butter Pickles

4 qts cucumbers (the pickling kind), sliced about ¼-inch-thick
1 handful of salt
1 qt vinegar (not too sour)
2 cups sugar
1 tsp ground mustard
1 tsp black pepper
½ tsp turmeric
1 dozen onions, sliced

Cover cucumbers with salt and boiling water and let stand overnight. Add vinegar, sugar, spices, and onions, and bring this mixture to a boil for no more than 3 minutes. Place in bottles and seal.

Barrie Smith's Green Tomato Pickles

1 dozen mangos (bell peppers, chopped fine)
6 onions, sliced
½ peck green tomatoes (cored)
3 or 4 stalks celery (chopped fine)
vinegar
1 tsp turmeric
a little cinnamon

Put all the ingredients in salt water and light vinegar. Bring to a boil, then drain and let sit overnight. Return the ingredients to the kettle. Cover with vinegar, and add sugar to taste along with the turmeric and cinnamon. Bring to a boil and then seal in jars.

Being "canned," meant being dismissed from service.

Dill Pickles

60 small pickling cucumbers (wash, dry & slice thin but do not pare)
5 cents worth of black mustard seed
5 cents worth of yellow mustard seed
½ cup of salt
1 cup of olive oil
1 Tbsp of celery seed
½ cup of granulated sugar dissolved in in 1 qt of vinegar

Put in all ingredients in a stone crock and mix together.

We love this recipe for its list of ingredients in the amount spent at the local grocery store. But you'll need to refer to your favorite guide for pickling.

Syracuse Pickles

4 qts sliced cucumber
4 large onions, sliced thin and uniform
3 red peppers, sliced thin and uniform
salt
vinegar
3 cups sugar
4 Tbsp white mustard seed
1 tsp turmeric
1 tsp cloves

Cover the cucumber, onions and peppers with salt, and let stand overnight. Drain, then pour just enough vinegar over them to cover. Bring to a quick boil and then bottle and seal.

> Today's table salt contains anti-caking compounds to keep it from clumping.
>
> Pickling and canning salts do not have these additives.
>
> Historically, salt was stored in wooden containers and hung by the hearth to protect it from dampness.

Putting vegetables in a salty brine draws the water out, increasing the "crunch" factor in the pickle. It also protects against microorganisms. However, there is a balance. The cooks in this kitchen knew their own by practice. For your own canning, refer to modern recipes for specific instructions.

Mrs. May Barnes' Pickles

6 qts cucumber, (sliced, but not fine)
Onions and mangos to suit (mangos are bell peppers)
5 cups sugar
3 cups vinegar
1 cup water
1 tsp of cinnamon
1 tsp of turmeric

Bring the sugar, water, and vinegar to a boil and let simmer for 15 minutes. Add the rest of the ingredients and bring to a boil again. Add salt to taste. Then put into canning jars and seal.

Carrie Ovendorf's Heinz Pickles

cucumbers
1 gallon vinegar
1 cup horseradish (grated)
½ cup salt
½ cup mustard
1 cup sugar
5 cents worth of saccharine

You may be forced to double it, if not sweet enough.

The Heinz Company

The Heinz Company was started by Henry J. Heinz in the late 1800s in Pennsylvania.
Given the list of ingredients here, it is interesting to note that horseradish was one of the first products Henry sold. His second was ketchup.
Henry Heinz helped pioneer sanitary techniques for food processing.

We love how this recipe shows the increasing availability of ingredients in small-town America. In this recipe, we believe Mrs. Kennedy is giving saccharine a try, which is used as a substitute for sugar. But you'll notice sugar is also listed in the ingredients. Is this a sure-sign of testing a product without wanting to deal with the waste of food and effort from failure? One can sense her doubts in the recipe through her suggestion of doubling it, if it is "not sweet enough."

Mixed Pickles
Chow-Chow

50 small cucumbers	2 lbs sugar
1 head cabbage	5 cents turmeric
2 heads cauliflower	5 cents celery seed
3 heads celery	5 cents black pepper seed
2 qts small green onions	2 red peppers
1 lb mustard (ground)	vinegar

Cut your cucumbers in pieces. If you are dealing with large, soft cucumbers instead of small ones, throw a strong brine over them for one day or night, then put in light alum water overnight to harden them.

Set the cucumbers in vinegar for 1 day, and then they will be ready for your chow-chow.

Chop the celery, cabbage, and cauliflower. Keep the onions whole and put them all in salt water that is *strong enough to float an egg*. Then drain overnight in a colander and they will be ready for the dressing.

Bring about 1 quart of vinegar to a boil and mix the mustard into it. Continue boiling until it thickens. Add the remaining spices, cabbage, cauliflower, celery and cucumbers; and jar while it is hot. Seal up tight.

Mrs. Jones's
Pickled Corn

Peel and cook the corn for 10 minutes in boiling water. Cut the corn from the cob and let it cool thoroughly. For each quart of corn, add 1 teacup of salt, layering it in the crock until the crock is full.

Adding salt to water increases its density. The kitchen tip in the chow-chow recipe is priceless! How can you tell if your water is salty enough? If you can float an egg, of course!

Best Canned Corn

4 ½ cups corn
½ cup sugar
¾ cup water
¼ cup salt

Boil the corn until tender, then cut the corn from the cobs and mix with the remaining ingredients. If canned corn comes out too salty, rinse before using.

a note on tomatoes

Tomatoes were not always prized in kitchens. Initially, people believed they were poisonous because they are related to deadly nightshade, and the smaller fruits resemble the nightshade berries. Moreover, the Latin name for tomatoes translates as "wolf peach" because in folklore the fruit is used to kill werewolves.

Tomatoes were not widely eaten until the late 1800s as word spread from public demonstrations showing they were safe.

Recipes for green tomatoes likely reigned in climates where a short growing season did not allow the fruit to vine-ripen before frost. Or perhaps, people ate green tomatoes to be safe and avoid the "poisonous" red ones.

To "cut" was to uncouple one car from another.

5 MAIN DISHES & SIDES

It may seem surprising that this chapter is not overflowing with recipes. However, experienced cooks grew up helping prepare the main meals for the table and often knew how to put them together. Meals were often centered around breads, soups, stews and pot roasts where meats, vegetables, and spices were cooked together over a fire or put in a hot oven until done. Preparing meals in this way was second nature, much in the way that any activity done daily does not need instructions once it is learned. This approach and way of life is shown in the newspaper clipping that was kept tucked in the journal. The author of the insert felt that anything served at her restaurant, such as creamed eggs, pocketbook rolls, cream puffs, and broiled halibut, could be made by anyone. But we are sure that did not keep people from eating at her establishment.

As grocery stores opened and brought an increasing availability of foods such as rice, gelatin, commercially canned products such as horseradish and olives, vegetable oils, and other worldly spices, learning to cook with them lead to a sharing of recipes. The recipes in this chapter such as corn bisque, fritters, and pan-fried croquettes provide evidence of this progression.

Daily Menu

There isn't anything here you cannot make if you have ever made anything at all, and besides when this menu was written the rain was drizzling down and the atmosphere was cold and miserable, and altogether nobody was happy. So we offer you a recipe for ginger apples, which are every bit as good, if not better, than spiced peaches or pears.

Breakfast
Cereal. Fruit. Milk
Creamed eggs. Stewed potatoes
Pocketbook Rolls
Coffee

Lunch
Panned oysters. Toasted biscuits
Cream puffs. Tea

Dinner
Tomato soup. Broiled halibut
Creamed cabbage
Mashed potatoes. Cucumber salad
Cheese toast. Spice jelly
Coffee

Ginger apples ~ Make a syrup of 4 pounds of sugar and 1 pint of water as the foundation for one of the most delicious apple relishes. As soon as the syrup boils up, add 1 ounce of green ginger sliced. Put in also the yellow rind of 4 lemons cut as thin strips and chopped fine, then add 4 pounds of apples, pared and quartered. Sweet apples are best. Cook for 20 minutes and then add the strained juice of 4 lemons. Let it come to a boil again. Pour into jars and seal.

Salad

Shred cabbage and lettuce leaves, then add grated carrot on top. Add few walnut meats, and if you like, stuffed olives. Top with a drop of mayonnaise.

Vegetable Salad

1 cup shredded cabbage
1 cup celery (diced)
2 cucumbers (sliced)
3 tomatoes (chopped)
1 red pepper, fresh or canned
2 green peppers (cut fine)

1 tsp salt
1 tsp paprika
1 Tbsp sugar
1 Tbsp vinegar
3 Tbsp olive oil

Mix all together and serve cold.

This salad goes fine with fish or cold meats. If you have no celery, double the amount of cabbage and add 1 teaspoon celery salt.

Christmas Salad

1 stalk celery (diced)
1 can sliced pineapple
½ green pepper (chopped fine)
1 pt cottage cheese
¾ cup mayonnaise

1 can pimento
1 ½ cups pecans
1 envelope of Knox gelatin
½ pt whipping cream
¼ cup sugar

Drain and reserve juice of pineapple. Heat the juice and mix it with the gelatin. Let the gelatin cool, then add the other ingredients, including a pinch of salt, cottage cheese, mayonnaise and the cream which has been whipped with the sugar. Put in a tray and let set.

A "turntable" operates on a pivot for diverting cars to another track.

a note on gelatin

Gelatin has been used for 100s of years, but obtaining it was a long and tedious process that involved boiling beef bones and hooves. (Yes, housewives did this!)

Believe it or not, the powdered gelatin we use today has historic ties to the railroad. In 1845 Peter Cooper, inventor of the steam locomotive, received his patent for powdered gelatin.

In 1890 Charles Knox began making and distributing powdered gelatin through his company.... Recognize the name?

Tomato Salad

12 large sized tomatoes (peeled, cored, and sliced)
3 hard-boiled eggs
1 raw egg, well-beaten
1 tsp salt
½ tsp cayenne pepper
1 tsp white sugar
2 Tbsp salad oil
2 Tbsp made mustard (prepared)
1 teacup vinegar

Rub the yolks to a smooth paste in a bowl. Add by degrees, the salt, pepper, sugar, mustard and oil. Beat the raw egg to a froth and stir in lastly the vinegar. Peel the tomatoes and slice them a quarter-inch thick. Set the dish on the ice while you are making the dressing. Stir a great lump of ice rapidly into the dressing until it is cold. Take the ice out and stir the dressing into the tomatoes. Set the salad back on the ice until you send it to the table.

Mrs. Hope's Tomato Chowder

1 peck ripe tomatoes
6 onions
5 mangos, red or green (bell peppers)
3 stalks celery
5 cups vinegar
2 lbs sugar
1 oz mustard seed
1 tsp celery seed
1 cup salt

Finely chop all the vegetables. Cover with salt, mix well, put in a colander and let drain overnight. Bring the sugar and vinegar to a boil and mix in mustard and celery seed, then can or bottle.

Delicious Corn Bisque

Corn bisque is delicious when made by heating a large can of creamy corn with 2 slices of onion and bacon that have been put through a grinder and combined with 3 cups of rich milk or part milk in cream. Garnish with paprika and minced parsley.

Buy the creamy corn for this, not the whole kernels.

Salmon Croquettes

2 cups of canned red salmon, minced
2 tsp onion juice
1 tsp salt
3 eggs
¾ cup cracker crumbs
¼ cup evaporated milk

Mix the first four ingredients well and let stand for 15 minutes. Shape into little cakes. Dip them in cracker crumbs and sauté gently in a ½ inch of melted butter in a frying pan until browned. Serve piping hot with tartar sauce.

Salmon Croquettes

1 can (cold) of boiled salmon
1 tsp salt
1 Tbsp chopped parsley
juice of ½ lemon
a little cayenne
1 cup cream
1 Tbsp butter
3 Tbsp flour

    Finely chop the salmon and add to it the salt, parsley, lemon juice, and cayenne. Mix thoroughly. Put the cream on to boil, but be sure not to scorch. Rub butter and flour together in a small bowl until smooth, then stir it into the boiling cream and cook for 2 minutes. Season lightly. Now stir this mixture into the salmon and mix well. Turn out on a dish to cool. When cool, form mixture into cork-shaped croquettes. Roll them in a beaten egg, followed by bread crumbs and fry in boiling fat.

Rice Croquettes

1 cup raw rice
1 tsp salt
1 egg (yolk only)
1 pint of water
cracker crumbs

    Place rice in a granite kettle, add the salt and water, and cook until tender (15 or 20 minutes). Stir often and add more water as needed. Do not cook too long though, as rice will be hard to handle. Drain well in a colander. If water is very thick and starchy, throw water over the rice and wash it clean. When cool enough to handle, add the beaten yolk of the egg. Stir well and add a seasoning of salt. Form the rice into cylinders. Roll each in the beaten egg, then in cracker crumbs (ground up like dust), and fry in deep fat. The fat should be very hot, so that the outside of the croquettes will crust over at once. Do not cover them in the kettle. When brown, drain on yellow paper and serve at once.

Ham Croquettes

1 cup of finely chopped cooked ham
1 cup bread crumbs
1 cup hot mashed potatoes
1 Tbsp butter
3 eggs, beaten (1 reserved for dipping before frying)
a little pepper

Mix all the ingredients together. When cool enough to handle, form into croquettes, then dip in the beaten egg and roll in bread crumbs. Deep fry until brown and crispy. Drain and serve.

Cucumber Fritters

Peel and grate full-grown cucumbers. Press all the juice from the pulp and add the juice to 1 quart of the pulp, ½ teacup of rich sweet cream, and ½ pint flour. Add salt and pepper to taste. Beat 4 eggs until they are very light and add them to a bit of melted butter, which should be very thick. Stir this into the pulp batter. Have a kettle of boiling lard ready. Drop the batter in one large spoonful at a time. Remove the fritter as soon as it is crisp and brown. Serve as you would fried oysters, which they very much resemble.

A "Ham" was a student telegrapher.

American Chop Suey

1 pound of Hamburger Steak, ground
3 medium sized onions
1 bunch of celery
1 Tbsp lard
1 Tbsp butter
1 box spaghetti or macaroni
2 or 3 cans of tomato soup or chili sauce* (*recipe on page 20*)
1 tsp salt
¼ tsp pepper

Chop onion and celery together, not fine but medium. Add these to the meat. Mix thoroughly and add salt and pepper. Put lard and butter in a frying pan over medium-high heat. Add the meat mixture and fry for about 20 minutes until done, stirring often. While the meat is frying, prepare the spaghetti or macaroni by boiling it in salted water until tender. Drain the pasta and add this to the meat mixture. Stir in the tomato soup, then put the mixture in a baking dish and bake ¾ hour in a hot oven.

And if that's good, I say it is.

Scalloped Cheese

In a buttered baking dish, alternate bread crumbs with thin slices of cheese. Prior to layering, add celery salt or chopped celery and pepper. Cover with a ½ pint of rich cream mixed with a well-beaten egg. Dollop with pieces of butter. Bake in a hot oven.

Whoever likes cheese will surely enjoy it in this way.

Meat Loaf

2 cups finely chopped meat
2 eggs
1 cup milk
2 Tbsp shortening
1 tsp baking powder
pinch of salt, pepper, and cloves
flour (enough to stiffen)

Mix all ingredients together and put in a pan and bake in a hot oven. When done, let cool. When cool, slice and dip in a batter made of a little milk and a beaten egg. Fry in lard.

English Veal Loaf

Boil in as little water as possible four pounds of shoulder. Allow to cool, and chop fine. Mix the following into the chopped meat: two eggs, salt, pepper, sage, one cup cracker crumbs, one cup of the liquid that the meat was boiled in, and 2 tablespoons of butter. (Do not omit the sage.) Press this mixture into a loaf pan (not tin, but granite) and bake slowly for 25 minutes, but do not brown. (Loaf should be quite moist when put in the oven.) After baking, set on ice for several hours.

Meats were hung from a "beef rail" near a car's ceiling.

Chicken Salad

1 roasted chicken, cut in dice-sized pieces
celery, chopped in an amount equal to the chicken
whites of 6 hard-boiled eggs
salt & pepper to taste

3 raw eggs, well-beaten
1 Tbsp yellow mustard
10 Tbsp melted butter
12 Tbsp sharp vinegar
salt & Cayenne pepper

Mix the first four ingredients together in a large bowl and set aside. Rub the yolks of 6 hard-boiled eggs into a paste and add the mustard that has been dissolved in a little bit of water, the butter, vinegar and salt and pepper, and mix well. Bring this mixture to a boil and beat until very light. Pour this mixture over the celery and chicken. Serve when ready.

Chicken Salad

Cut the white meat (and dark meat if you like it) of a roasted chicken into small bits that are the size of peas. Chop an equal amount of celery nearly as fine. Also chop the white of 3 hard-boiled eggs. Mix these together and set aside.

For the dressing, rub the yolks of 3 hard-boiled eggs into a smooth paste. Add 1½ teaspoons of mustard, a 1½ teaspoons of salt, 3 tablespoons of oil, and a wine glass of vinegar. Mix well and add a little cream.

Add the dressing to the chicken and celery mixture when ready to serve.

6 DESSERTS

Many of the dessert, cookie, and sweet bread recipes in the cookery journal consisted only of a list of ingredients and minimal instructions, as the chef who used them in the kitchen knew what to do with her wood or coal-fired oven. In general, cookies are baked in today's ovens at 375 degrees. Cakes and muffins tend to be baked at 350 degrees, while sweet breads range from 325 to 375 degrees. At the very least, using these recipes should be approached as an adventure. It is my hope that they will give you fresh ideas on how to modify some of your personal recipes, or coax you in to trying an old idea in a new way in your own home.

It should be noted that many of these recipes call for milk. Sour milk was kept on hand for baking. Sweet milk referred to milk that was fresh. When buttermilk or heavy cream were used, they are specified.

A "brownie" was a demerit for a rule violation.

Lemon Pie

grated rind [zest] of 2 lemons and juice
1 cup sugar
½ cup molasses
½ cup hot water
2 eggs, beaten
1 Tbsp melted butter
1 Tbsp flour

Mix ingredients and pour into a pie pan [lined with dough]. Bake in a moderate oven until set.

Sour Cream Pie

1 cup sour cream
1 cup raisins
1 cup sugar
1 egg
1 Tbsp cornstarch
2 Tbsp vinegar

Put raisins through the food chopper. Mix all together and bake in a hot oven [in a pie pan lined with pie dough] until set.

Crumb Pie

1 cup sugar
3 cups flour
1 tsp baking soda, divided
½ cup butter, softened
1 cup syrup
1 cup hot water
2 eggs

Mix the flour, ½ teaspoon baking soda, butter, and sugar together until crumbly. Take out 1 cup of this mixture, then divide the remaining balance of the first mixture and put in two crusts. Heat the syrup, water, and the remaining soda together in a pan, let cool, beat in eggs, then pour this mixture over the top of the first in the pie pans. Sprinkle the remaining crumb mixture over the top and bake.

This recipe sounds like shoofly pie, which uses brown sugar and molasses.

Graham Cracker Crust

17 graham crackers rolled fine
½ cup melted butter
½ cup confectioner's sugar

Combine ingredients and press it in a pie pan for a crust. Then make a cream filling [*see below*], cover with a meringue [*see Orange Cream Pie*], and sprinkle the top with cracker dust. Bake.

Cream Pie

1 qt milk
3 Tbsp sugar
2 Tbsp flour

2 Tbsp butter, melted
3 eggs
vanilla to taste

This is to be baked with a bottom crust. Beat egg whites to a froth. Add sugar. Mix remaining ingredients and fold in. Spread over the crust and bake until lightly browned.

Orange Cream Pie

2 eggs, divided
1 cup sugar, divided
1 heaping Tbsp flour
1 heaping Tbsp cornstarch
1 pt milk
Elsinov Extract of Orange to taste

Beat the eggs yolks thoroughly with ½ cup sugar. Add flour and cornstarch dissolved in a little milk. Add this to the remaining milk with the yolk mixture, bring to a boil and let it cook about 3 minutes. After milk has cooled, flavor it with orange extract and pour into a baked crust.

Beat the whites of 2 eggs until stiff. Fold in the ½ cup of sugar and orange extract and spread on top of pie. Put it in a moderate oven and let it brown slightly.

Katherine Caldwell's Pineapple Sponge

1 Tbsp gelatin
¼ cup cold water
2/3 cup boiling water
2/3 cup sugar
Grated rind [zest] of ¼ lemon
juices of two lemons
½ cup of drained grated pineapple
2 egg whites, beaten to froth and folded in

Spanish Cream

1 Tbsp gelatin
¼ cup milk
2 ¾ cup milk
1/8 tsp salt

½ cup sugar
3 eggs, separated
1 tsp vanilla

Soften the gelatin in the ¼ cup milk. Add the remaining milk, sugar, and salt and place mixture in a double boiler. Heat until milk is scalded. Beat egg yolks slightly and ½ cup of the hot milk mixture. Stir the egg yolk-milk mixture into the milk in the double boiler. Cook until slightly thickened, stirring constantly. Remove from heat and let cool until warm. Beat the egg whites until stiff and fold into the warm mixture with the vanilla. Turn into a dish or molds and chill until firm.

Pop Corn Pudding

Pop some corn nicely and then roll it as fine as you can. Mix 1 pint of the corn with 1 quart of sweet milk. Add a small piece of melted butter and 1 teaspoon salt. Beat 2 eggs with enough sugar to sweeten the milk. Mix all together and bake for 20 minutes.

> Sweet milk refers to fresh milk that isn't sour, like buttermilk, which was kept on-hand for baking.

Lemon Rice Pudding

1 cup rice
1 cup water
1 qt milk
pinch salt
lemon rind grated [zest]
½ cup sugar

Boil the rice and water together until the water is absorbed (about 7 minutes). Then add the remaining ingredients to the pot and bring to a boil again. Let simmer on back of the stove for 30 minutes. Put into molds, let cool, and chill.

Peach Pudding

1 egg
1 ½ cups sugar
3 Tbsp melted butter
1 cup sweet milk
1 ½ cup flour
1 ½ tsp baking powder
2 cups of peaches, put through a grinder

Beat the egg, sugar, and butter together. Mix in the milk, flour and baking powder until smooth. Fold in the peaches. Turn into molds and bake.

Wampsie Pudding

Mix 1 pint sour cream with a little soda and enough flour to form a batter. Fill a pan with sliced baking apples, but don't place them too close together so that they are packed. Pour the batter over the apples and bake until light brown. Eat with cream and sugar.

> The name of this recipe may refer to the Native American Wampanoag tribe from the Massachusetts area in early America.
>
> The first American best-selling book, "The Sovereignty and Goodness of God," was written by Mary Rowlandson about her captivity by Wampanoags.

Rhubarb Custard

1 cup of rhubarb (cut fine)
1 cup of sugar
1 cup of milk
2 eggs
1 Tbsp cornstarch
small piece of butter

    Scald the milk. Mix the sugar, cornstarch and melted butter into a little bit of milk to make a paste. Mix some of the hot milk into the paste. Stirring slowly, add the rest of the hot milk to the paste, until thickened. Beat the eggs and add slowly, stirring into to the custard. Cook for a couple minutes, and stir in the rhubarb. Turn into molds and chill until set.

Cup Custard

1 qt milk
½ cup sugar
4 eggs
¼ of a grated nutmeg

    Beat the eggs until light, then then add the sugar and beat again. Add the milk and nutmeg and stir until sugar is dissolved. Pour into custard cups. Place the cups in a pan of boiled water, and then put the pan in the oven. Bake until the custard is set, then set in a cool place. When cold, serve.

Cottage Pudding

1 cup sugar
1 cup milk
1 egg
1 Tbsp butter
1 tsp baking powder

    Mix these ingredients with 2 cups flour and bake as a loaf cake. Eat with sauce. [*Suggestion: Hard Sauce, page 19.*]

Snowball Custard

Beat the whites of 3 eggs until moderately stiff. Dip them by the tablespoonful into one pint of boiling milk. As they rise, turn them, and when done, put them in a pudding dish. Then beat the yolks and sweeten to taste. Put the sweetened yolks into the milk and stir until it thickens. Remove from the fire and flavor with lemon. Turn this custard into a glass dish and lay the boiled egg whites on top.

Smear Cheese Cake Pie

2 cups smear cheese (cream cheese)
2 cups milk
2 eggs (beaten)
½ cup sugar
½ tsp salt
Sprinkle cinnamon on top.

Mix ingredients together, turn into a pie shell, and bake in a moderate oven until set.

You may want to add a little bit of flour to help set the batter.

Smear cheese referred to a spreadable cheese. This term was derived from the German word, "schmier."

Blanche A's Spice Cake

1 lb brown sugar
1 cup butter and lard, mixed
3 eggs
1 cup sour milk
1 tsp baking soda

1 tsp cream of tartar
1 ½ tsp cinnamon
1 tsp cloves
3 cups flour

I usually use 2 ½ cups flour with better results, but of course use your own judgment.

Hot Milk Sponge

4 eggs
2 cups sugar
1 cup hot milk
2 cups flour, mixed with 2 tsp baking powder
1 tsp vanilla

Save out the white of one egg for icing. Beat eggs until foamy, then add sugar and continue beating until thick and lemony in color. Add milk and vanilla. Quickly beat in flour mixture. [*Bake in a 10-inch tube pan at 350 degrees until top springs back lightly when pressed.*]
Drizzle with a light icing.

White Layer Cake

2 cups sugar
1 cup butter and lard scant
1 cup water
3 cups flour
2 tsp baking powder
whites of 6 eggs
flavoring

Be sure and sift sugar.

> Until 1870 all flour was stone-ground; by 1880 mill stones had been replaced with steel, iron, or porcelain rollers.
>
> Flour was initially put in 198-pound barrels. The sewing machine paved the way for the use of cotton sacks. The 50-pound "pillow" sacks were the most popular size in the early 1900s.

Lemon Cream

Grated rind [*zest*] and juice of 2 lemons
½ cup of butter
1 cup sugar
6 eggs

Beat the eggs until very light. Melt the butter, sugar, and lemon juice together. Stir in the eggs slowly and bring the mixture to a boil for a few minutes, stirring constantly. Let cool and spread on a cake as you would jelly.

Angel Food Cake

Beat the white of eleven eggs with one level teaspoon of cream of tartar until stiff and dry. Fold in lemon extract, 1 ½ cup sugar and 1 ¼ cup flour that have each been sifted 3 times.

> Elizabeth Shade Kennedy had assistants in her kitchen. Many recipes in her journal were transcribed by "Blanche." Some seem to have been written by someone who was watching them be prepared. Others are styled as if for later use by another, an assistant perhaps, who would be using the journal.

Angel Food Cake

Whites of 13 eggs
1 large tumbler of flour
1 lb granulated sugar
1 tsp cream of tartar
1 tsp vanilla

Make this cake in the same pan you mix it in. Sift your flour and sugar 4 times. Bake in a moderate oven for 40 minutes.

Sponge Cake

Beat the yolks of 4 eggs with 3 tablespoons of water until thick and lemon colored. Gradually stir in 1 cup of sifted sugar and beat for 2 minutes.

Put 1 ½ tablespoons of cornstarch in a cup. Fill the cup with milk. Sift flour with 1 ¼ teaspoons of baking powder and ¼ teaspoon of salt. Stir all these ingredients together. When thoroughly mixed, add the whites of 4 eggs that have been beaten until stiff and 1 teaspoon of lemon extract.

Bake for 30 minutes in a moderate oven.

Let Blanche copy these — they are all fine.

Banana Cake

1 whole egg
yolks of 2 eggs
1 cup sugar
1 cup sweet milk
2 ¼ cup flour
Butter, the size of an egg
2 tsp baking powder

For filling, beat the whites of 2 eggs to a stiff froth. Add sugar and 4 sliced bananas, or enough to cover with the batter. Bake in a moderate oven.

White Mountain Cake

1 cup butter
2 cups sugar
1 cup sweet milk
4 eggs
1 tsp cream of tartar
2 tsp baking soda
Juice and grated rind of 1 lemon
Flour, enough to thicken (3 cups)

For Icing: Beat whites of 7 eggs to a stiff froth, then add 1 lb of icing [confectioner's] sugar. Spread each layer with icing then sprinkle over with sweetened coconut.

The White Mountain Cake was a three layer cake in which the layers were baked separately, whereas historically, other layer cakes were cut from a single baked layer and then stacked. White Mountain Cake was flavored with lemon. It has frosting between the layers, as well as over the whole cake.

Some historical recipes indicate cakes were set in a warm oven for a few minutes after the icing has been applied to allow it to set. Given the egg whites in this icing, this may be a consideration.

Ruth Grugan's Devil's Food Cake

2 cups sugar
½ cup butter
2 eggs, (separated)
¾ cup cocoa
½ cup hot water
2 cups flour
1 tsp baking soda dissolved in ½ cup buttermilk

Cream the butter and sugar, and then mix in the yolks of the eggs. Mix in the remaining ingredients and then fold in the beaten egg whites. Bake in a moderate oven.

Devil's Food

1 cup of brown sugar
¾ cup butter
1 ½ cup flour
2 eggs
½ cup sweet milk
1 tsp baking soda

Dark part to be boiled:
1 cup sugar
1 cup grated chocolate
1 cup sweet milk

Bring the white sugar, chocolate, and milk to a boil in a pan. Stir and heat until smooth. Let cool. Mix the remaining ingredients together and add to the chocolate milk. Mix the batter thoroughly and bake in a moderate oven.

Rachel's Black Chocolate Cake

2 cups sugar
2/3 cup butter
2 ½ cup flour
4 eggs

1 cup sweet milk
2 ½ tsp baking powder
½ cup Bakers chocolate
1 tsp vanilla

Icing

Boil 2 cups sugar with ½ cup sweet milk together for 3 minutes, then beat until cooled.

Maggy Brown's Oatmeal Cake

2 cups brown sugar
2 cups oatmeal
½ cup shortening
½ cup boiling water

1 tsp baking soda
1 Tbsp vanilla
flour to thicken
1 pinch of salt

Caramel Icing

1 ½ cups brown sugar
¾ cup milk

Butter, the size of egg

Boil 8 minutes or more.

Nancy Lee's Cup Cakes

4 eggs
2 cups sugar
2 cups pastry flour
1 ½ tsp baking powder

1 cup milk
4 Tbsp butter
1 tsp vanilla

Beat eggs for 10 minutes with a rotary egg beater. Add sugar slowly and beat for 10 minutes more. Mix and sift the flour, baking powder together and add to the eggs and sugar. Bring the milk to a boil. Add the vanilla and butter and stir until butter is melted. Pour the milk into the first mixture, and stir well. Pour into a well-greased cup cake pan. Put in a hot oven (400 degrees) for 10 minutes, then reduce the temperature to 350 degrees and bake in a moderate oven for 25 minutes more or until done.

The batter appears very soft but this is correct. Fill pans only half-full, as cake rises before dough is firm.

Old Fashioned Jelly Roll

3/4 cup sifted Swans Down Cake Flour
3/4 teaspoon baking powder
3/4 teaspoon salt
4 eggs
3/4 cup sifted sugar
1 teaspoon vanilla
1 cup jelly (any flavor)

Sift flour once, measure. Combine baking powder, salt, and eggs in a bowl. Place over smaller bowl of hot water and beat with rotary egg beater, adding sugar gradually until mixture becomes thick and light-colored. Remove bowl from hot water. Fold in flour and vanilla. Turn into a greased pan, 15 x 10 inches, lined with greased paper, and bake in a hot oven (400 degrees) for 13 minutes.

Quickly cut off crisp edges of cake. Turn from pan at once on to a cloth covered with powdered sugar. Remove paper. Spread with jelly and roll. Wrap in cloth and cool on rack. (For moist butter sponge roll, fold 2 tablespoons of melted butter into batter before turning into pan.) All measurements are level.

Mab's Cake

2 cups sugar
½ cup butter
3 eggs
1 cup milk
3 cups flour
3 tsp baking powder

Ice Cream Cake

Whites of 4 eggs
1 cup butter
2 cups sugar
1 cup ice water
2 cups flour
1 cup cornstarch
2 tsp baking powder

Bake this cake in layers. When cool, spread softened ice cream on top of one layer and put second layer of cake on top. Refreeze. Cover with frosting made from whipped cream, and chill again.

White Mound Cake

¾ cup shortening
1 ½ cups sugar
1 tsp almond extract
½ tsp vanilla extract

3 eggs
3 cups cake flour, sifted
3 ½ tsp baking powder
½ tsp salt

Cream the shortening thoroughly. Add the sugar slowly until it is thoroughly blended with the shortening. Beat the extracts into the shortening mixture. Add the eggs, one at a time, beating well after each addition. Sift the dry ingredients together. Add them to the shortening mixture alternately with milk. Bake in a well-greased pan or other heat-resistant container in a moderate oven (300 degrees).

Royal Strawberry Cake

1 cup sugar
4 Tbsp shortening
1 egg
2 cups flour
3 teaspoons baking powder
1/8 tsp salt
1 cup milk
1 tsp vanilla

½ pint heavy cream
1 qt strawberries

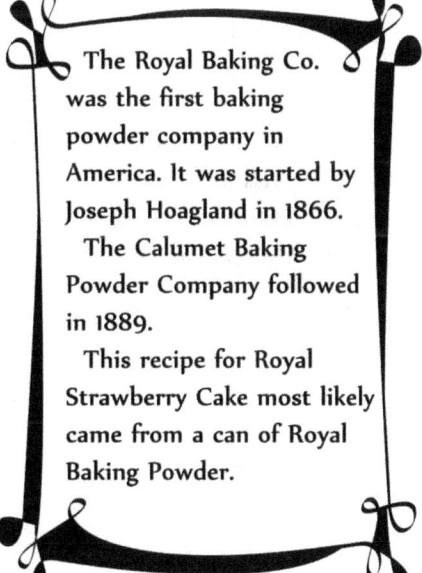

The Royal Baking Co. was the first baking powder company in America. It was started by Joseph Hoagland in 1866.
The Calumet Baking Powder Company followed in 1889.
This recipe for Royal Strawberry Cake most likely came from a can of Royal Baking Powder.

Cream sugar and shortening together. Add the beaten egg. Add part of the flour, baking powder and salt, which have been sifted together. Then add part of the milk. Mix well, and add the remaining flour. Add the remaining milk and vanilla flavoring. Bake in a shallow greased pan for 20 or 30 minutes.

When cooled, split the cake layer in half. Whip the cream, sweetening with confectioner's sugar, if desired.

Spread whipped cream and crushed sweetened strawberries on the bottom layer. Place the second layer on top of the strawberries, then cover the top layer with whipped cream and whole strawberries.

Marshmallow Gold Cake

2 cups sifted Swans Down Cake Flour
2 teaspoons Calumet Baking Powder
1/2 cup butter or other shortening
1/4 teaspoon salt
1 cup sugar
3 egg yolks, very well beaten
3/4 cup milk
1 teaspoon vanilla

Sift flour once, measure, add baking powder and salt and sift 3 times. Cream shortening, add sugar gradually, and cream together until fluffy. Add egg yolks and beat well. Add flour alternately with milk in small amounts, beating after each addition until smooth. Add vanilla and beat again. Bake in two greased 8-inch layer pans in a moderate oven (375 degrees) for 25 to 30 minutes.

Marshmallow lemon frosting: Make seven-minute frosting, using 2 egg whites, 1 cup sugar, 1 tablespoon water and 3 tablespoons lemon juice. Flavor with 1/2 teaspoon grated lemon rind. Fold in 16 marshmallows, quartered. Spread between layers and over cake.

Coconut Cake

1 cup butter
3 cups sugar
1 cup sweet milk with 1 tsp baking soda dissolved
1 tsp cream of tartar
5 eggs
4 cups flour
1 cup sweetened coconut

Mix the butter and sugar together until creamy. Slowly stir in the other ingredients. Bake in a moderate oven.

Silver and Gold Cake

Silver layers:
Whites of 8 eggs, beaten to a froth
1 cup of butter
2 cups of sugar
1 cup of buttermilk
1 tsp baking soda
1 tsp cream of tartar
4 cups flour

Gold layers:
Yolks of 8 eggs, beaten
1 cup of butter
2 cups of sugar
1 cup of buttermilk
1 tsp baking soda
1 tsp cream of tartar
4 cups flour

Mix the ingredients together for each of the cake layers. Bake in 9-inch pans in a moderate oven. When cooled, stack the cake layers alternating between silver and gold, spreading a frosting between each layer and over the top of the cake.

Marble Cake

Light Part:
Whites of 7 eggs
2 cups sugar
1 cup milk
1 cup butter
Flour, enough to thicken
1 tsp baking soda dissolved in a little milk
2 tsp cream of tartar

Dark Part:
Yolks of 7 eggs
2 cups brown sugar
2 cups molasses
1 cup butter
1 cup buttermilk
Flour, enough to thicken
1 tsp nutmeg
2 tsp cloves
2 tsp cinnamon
2 tsp ginger
1 tsp baking soda

Drop a spoonful of each batter alternately into a well-greased cake pan. Try to drop it so that the cake will be well-streaked throughout, like a marble.

"King pin" was another name for the conductor.

Tip Top Cake

1 ½ cup sugar
1 cup sour milk (buttermilk)
3 eggs
2 ½ cups flour
1 Tbsp butter
1 tsp baking soda
1 tsp cream of tartar

Bake quickly in a hot oven.

Railroad Cake

1 cup white sugar
1 cup flour
3 eggs
butter, the size of an egg
1 tsp cream of tartar
½ tsp baking soda
essence [zest] of 1 lemon
a little milk

Bake in shallow greased pans in a hot oven. Batter will be thick.

Some published variations of this recipe suggest it was similar to Irish Soda Cake, but with raisins baked in it. However, the recipe presented here differs in that it is flavored with lemon and lacks raisins and is not similar to Irish Soda Cake. Instead, Mrs. Kennedy's recipe resembles vintage recipes published in "My Pet Recipes, Tried and True" and "Miss Parloa's New Cookbook" from the early 1900s.

The railroad cake recipe is believed to have originated with the railroad as passenger use became more popular and increased. One poster suggested that "travelers were obliged to buy bad coffee, railroad cakes, hardtack, and Sally Lunns from vendors who congregated at the stations along the way." One would surmise that it was not a highly regarded cake and prone to variation, as was the case in our search on its history. However, we are sure Mrs. Kennedy baked her cakes to a tasteful perfection.

7 COOKIES & TREATS

Raisin Cookies

2 cups sugar
½ cup lard
½ box raisins
1 tsp cinnamon
1 tsp ground cloves
pinch of salt
2 cups water
5 ½ cups flour mixed with 1 tsp of baking powder
2 eggs, beaten

Put the all the ingredients except the flour in a kettle and bring them to a boil for about 5 minutes. Set aside until cooled. Then add the flour, eggs, and nut meats, if desired. Bake in a moderate oven, about 350 degrees.

This can be baked as a loaf or drop cookies.

Helen Ovendorf's Cookies

3 eggs (beaten)
2 cups sugar
2/3 cup butter
1 cup buttermilk
1 tsp baking soda
2 tsp baking powder
flour, enough to thicken dough

Mix the dry ingredients together and set aside. Mix the remaining ingredients together and then combine with the dry ingredients. Bake as drop cookies in a moderate oven on a lightly greased baking sheet until done.

Blanche's Ginger Cookies

2 cups molasses
1 cup brown Sugar
1 cup lard
1 cup boiling water
2 tsp baking soda
1 tsp ginger
1 tsp cinnamon
flour, enough to stiffen dough

Mix at night, and let set until following morning, then bake in a moderate oven on a lightly greased baking sheet.

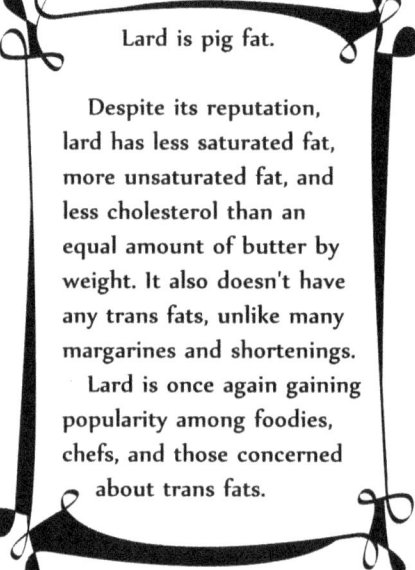

Lard is pig fat.

Despite its reputation, lard has less saturated fat, more unsaturated fat, and less cholesterol than an equal amount of butter by weight. It also doesn't have any trans fats, unlike many margarines and shortenings.

Lard is once again gaining popularity among foodies, chefs, and those concerned about trans fats.

Cookies

2 cups sugar
¾ cup lard
½ cup buttermilk
1 tsp baking soda
2 eggs
flavor with nutmeg
flour, enough to make dough middling stiff

Bake on a lightly greased baking sheet in a moderate oven.

Lemon Cookies

2 cups sugar
½ cup butter
2 eggs
1 lemon grated rind and juice
½ tsp cream tartar
flour, enough to moderately stiffen (about 2 ½ cups)
½ tsp baking soda
2 Tbsp milk

Chill the dough for an hour. Roll out the dough and cut with a cookie cutter. Place them on a lightly greased baking sheet and bake at 375 for about 8 minutes until lightly set.

These brought the idea of lemon snaps to mind, and would be wonderful with a cup of tea.

Esther Bullick's Drop Cookies

Recipe #1
2 cups sugar
1 cup lard butter
½ cup water
3 cups flour, enough to stiffen
½ cup sweet milk
2 eggs
3 tsp baking powder
flavoring

Recipe #2
2 cups sugar
1 cup lard
1 cup milk
2 eggs
2 tsp baking powder
½ tsp baking soda
flavoring
flour, enough to stiffen

Mix ingredients together and bake in a moderate oven on a lightly greased baking sheet until set.

A "dinky" was a small engine used at shops and roundhouses for switching cars.

Mrs. Walter Barnes' Cookies

1 cup white sugar
1 cup brown sugar
1 cup sour cream
3 eggs
1 cup lard
1 tsp baking soda
2 tsp baking powder
1 pinch salt
1 Tbsp vanilla
cloves
flour, enough to stiffen

Mix ingredients together and bake in a moderate oven on a lightly greased baking sheet until set.

Cookies

2 pts sugar
1 pt lard
1 pt sweet milk
3 eggs
1 Tbsp vanilla
5 cents hartshorn
flour, enough to stiffen

Mix ingredients together and bake in a moderate oven on a lightly greased baking sheet until set.

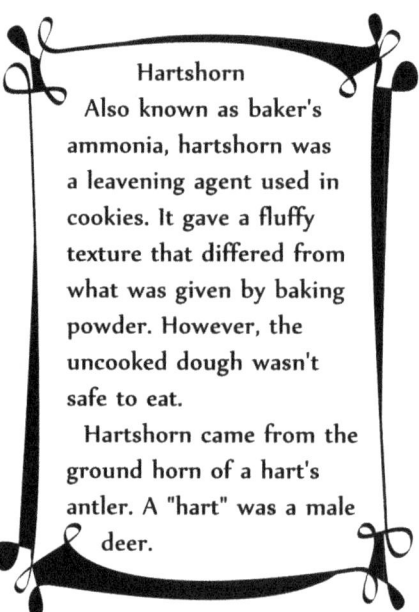

Hartshorn
Also known as baker's ammonia, hartshorn was a leavening agent used in cookies. It gave a fluffy texture that differed from what was given by baking powder. However, the uncooked dough wasn't safe to eat.

Hartshorn came from the ground horn of a hart's antler. A "hart" was a male deer.

Baking powder which is activated by moisture instead of heat can be used as a substitute for hartshorn.

Ginger Snaps

2 eggs
2 cups sugar
1 pt molasses
1 pt lard
1 cup water
1 ½ tsp baking powder
1 Tbsp vinegar
pinch salt
2 Tbsp ginger
flour, enough to make dough very stiff

Mix ingredients together. Roll, cut, and bake.

Cream Puffs

1 cup sifted flour
1 cup water
½ cup butter
½ tsp salt
3 eggs
2 Tbsp sugar

    Put the water, butter, sugar and salt on the fire in a large sauce pan, and when the water begins to boil add the flour and sugar, stirring constantly while sifting it in. Continue to stir until the batter is perfectly smooth. Pour into a bowl to cool. When cool, add the unbeaten eggs, one at a time. Beat after each addition until smooth. Drop on a greased muffin tin. Bake in a hot oven. The puffs are done when they are split open on the top. This is where you will add the filling.

Cream Puff Filling

½ pint milk
1 egg (yolk only)
1 ½ Tbsp sugar
1 Tbsp cornstarch
½ tsp salt
2 tsp vanilla
½ tsp butter

    Place the yolk of an egg in a cup. Beat until light. Add 2 tablespoons of cold milk. Place cornstarch in another cup. Add same quantity of milk. When starch is dissolved, add the egg mixture. Place remaining milk and sugar on the fire in a double boiler. When boiling, stir in egg and cornstarch mixture. Stir until thick. Let boil for 3 minutes, then add vanilla. Let cool, then put a tablespoon in the top of each puff.

Egg Muffins

1 cup sugar
2 Tbsp butter
pinch salt
1 ½ cups sweet milk
2 Tbsp baking powder
3 eggs
Flour, enough to stiffen

    Bake these in a moderately hot oven in a greased cupcake tin.

Graham Muffins

1 pt sweet milk
a little salt
1 Tbsp molasses
2 cups graham flour
1 cup wheat flour
small piece of butter
2 tsp baking powder

    Bake these in a moderately hot oven in a greased cupcake tin.

Corn Cake

1 cup flour
1 cup yellow corn meal
¼ cup sugar
1 Tbsp melted butter
1 egg, beaten very light in a cup of milk
½ tsp salt
2 tsp baking powder

    Combine all ingredients and bake in a hot oven.

Peanut Butter Bread

2 cups of gluten flour
1 cup of white flour
1 cup of milk
1 cup peanut butter
½ cup sugar
1 cup egg
1 tsp salt
3 tsp baking powder
1 cup raisins

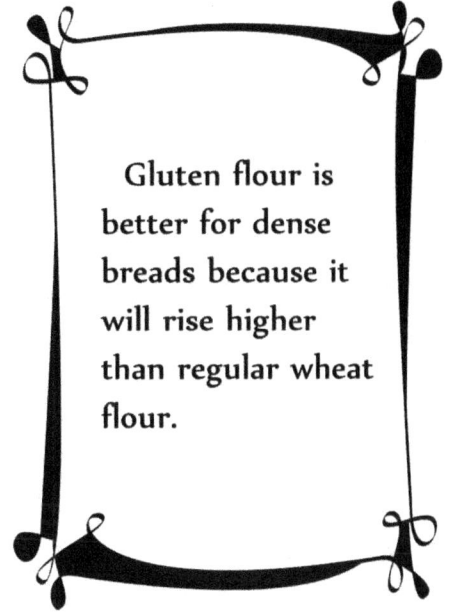

Gluten flour is better for dense breads because it will rise higher than regular wheat flour.

Coffee Fruit Cake

1 cup butter
1 cup brown sugar
2 cups raisins
¼ cup citron
1 large tsp ground cloves
1 large tsp allspice
1 egg

½ pint warm black coffee
1 cup molasses
3 cups flour
¾ lb currants
3 large tsp cinnamon
1 tsp baking powder

Frozen Cherries

3 cups canned cherries
2 cups sugar
2 cups water

Combine the sugar and water together and bring to a boil for three minutes. Put the cherries through a food chopper. When the sugar-water is cold, add the cherries and put in the freezer. Pack ice and salt around the mixture. Freeze until an emulsion is formed. Serve in ice cream glasses with a tiny flag on top.

Nancy Lee's Soft Gingerbread

1 cup brown sugar
½ cup butter
2 eggs
1 cup corn syrup
2 ½ cups flour
2 tsp cinnamon
1 tsp ginger
½ tsp salt
1 cup hot water or sweet milk
2 tsp baking soda

Cream the butter and sugar together. Add the well-beaten eggs and corn syrup. Sift the flour, cinnamon, ginger, salt, and baking soda together. Add the dry ingredients alternately with the hot water. Bake in a moderate oven (350 to 360 degrees).

Hickory Nut Cake

1 ½ cups sugar
½ cup butter
flour, enough to stiffen
whites of 3 eggs
1 cup milk
1 pound of brown sugar
1 cup of lard and butter, mixed
3 eggs
1 cup of buttermilk
2 tsp baking powder
1 tsp cream of tartar
1 ½ tsp of cinnamon
1 tsp cloves
3 cups flour
2 cups hickory nuts

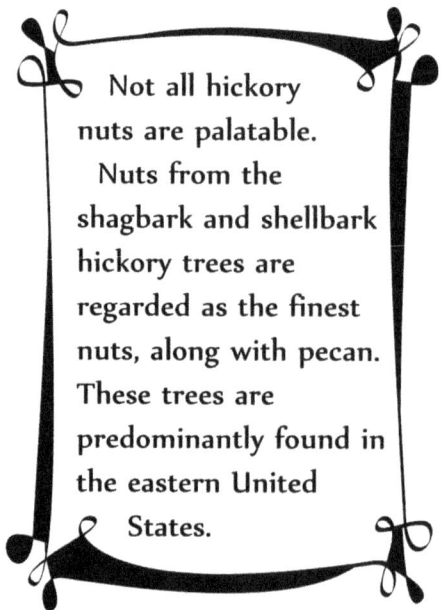

Not all hickory nuts are palatable. Nuts from the shagbark and shellbark hickory trees are regarded as the finest nuts, along with pecan. These trees are predominantly found in the eastern United States.

Fruit Cake

1 lb raisins
1 lb currants
½ lb figs
½ lb almonds
¼ lb citron
1 tsp nutmeg
½ cup butter

½ cup milk
2 cups flour
2 tsp cinnamon
2 tsp cloves
2 tsp baking powder
2 cups brown sugar
3 eggs

Ribbon Fruit Cake

Dark Part:
Yolks of 6 eggs
1 ½ cups sugar
1 cup butter
2 cups browned flour
1 ½ lb raisins
1 lb currents
½ lb citron
¼ lb nuts
2/3 cup whiskey
1 tsp of baking soda, dissolved in hot water
½ tsp cloves
½ tsp cinnamon
½ tsp nutmeg
½ tsp allspice

Light Part:
Whites of 6 eggs
1 cup white sugar
½ cup butter
½ cup sweet cream
2 ½ cups flour
2 heaping tsp baking powder
½ lb citron
1 lb almonds, chopped fine
½ cup grated coconut, chopped fine
1 tsp rose water
1 tsp lemon extract
1 small slice of sugared orange peel

Rose water is a fragrant water solution easily obtained through distillation of rose petals, which can be done at home with roses that have not been treated with pesticides and other chemicals. Adding rose water to cooked foods evokes the smell and taste of roses.

Rose water is not the same thing as essential rose oil, which is inedible.

Marshmallow Candy

2 tablespoons nuts
2 tablespoons cocoa
12 marshmallows

Soften the marshmallows in a double-boiler and stir in the cocoa and nuts. Drop from a spoon into another dish of more nuts that have been finely chopped, rolling the balls around until completely covered. Use a spoon for the process as the mixture is too soft to handle.

A little confectioners sugar added before dropping will make the mixture easier to handle.

Coconut Balls

Beat 1 egg white and stir in all the sweetened coconut possible so it will still hold together and keep moist. Shape into balls and roll in sweetened powdered cocoa.

Chocolate Caramels

½ cup butter
½ cup chocolate
1 cup brown sugar
1 cup molasses
1 cup sweet cream
flavor with vanilla

Cream Candy

3 cups sugar   Peppermint extract
1 cup water   Cream of tartar

Cook water and sugar until it crystallizes at the sides of the pan. Flavor with peppermint and a little bit of cream of tartar. Beat until creamy, and drop on oiled paper.

Popcorn Balls

3 qt of popped corn
1 cup molasses
½ cup sugar
½ cup water
2 Tbsp vinegar
1 Tbsp butter
¼ tsp soda

Mix the molasses, sugar, water, vinegar and butter together and cook over a moderate fire without stirring until a ball forms when a portion is turned into cold water. Add the soda and stir for a minute. Pour over the popped corn and allow to stand until cool enough to handle. Take up by the handful and press together in the palms of both hands to form balls.

Christmas Candy
Pineapple Delight

2 cups sugar
8 slices pineapple
1 cup water
1 cup shredded sweetened coconut

Boil the sugar and until it becomes brittle when dropped in cold water. Cut each slice pineapple in 4 quarters. Dip the fruit in the syrup and roll in the coconut. Set aside to cool.

A "gumshoe" was a railroad detective.

Panless Prunes

2 lb of dried prunes
1 cup of nut meats
2 tablespoon water
½ lb of candied cherries
1 cup powdered sugar
¼ teaspoon of maplene flavoring

Chop nut meats and candied cherries together. Steam the prunes for about 10 minutes. Let cool, then remove the pits by making just one incision on one side. Fill each prune with some of the nut and cherry mixture.

Mix the powdered sugar, water, and maplene into a moderately thick paste. Dip each prune in this mixture and lay aside on waxed paper to dry.

A Fast Set Dessert

Beat the whites of 2 eggs until stiff, then add a cup of freshly cooked applesauce (that has been cooled) and continue beating until well mixed and fluffy. Add a cup of chopped nut meats and set the mixture in the ice box to chill.
When ready to serve, garnish the dish with a sprinkling of sweetened coconut and dash of nutmeg.

Strawberry Cocktail

Use individual punch glasses. Slice 5 or 6 strawberries into each one. Cover the strawberries with the juice of an orange. Sprinkle with powdered sugar, and at the last minute add a tablespoon of shaved ice. Cover on a serving plate, then lift the cover as you are announcing the meal.

The compartment where ice was kept was called the ice bunker.

8 MEDICINALS & MISCELLANIES

For Gall Stones

Take 4 drops of turpentine 3 times a day for 3 days until you have taken it 9 times. Then stop and start in again. Take it only twice.

This is to be considered a historical reference only, not to be used for treatments of current ailments. The same applies to the rest of the tonics and remedies listed.

It is interesting to note that turpentine was documented in 1892 as a treatment for gallstones in a JAMA Medical Book.

Mathiglum

Take 4 pounds of honey and add 2 quarts of water for every pound. In this mixture, dissolve 2 pounds of brown sugar. Leave to stand and let the yeast work. When done working, pick off scum and cork tight.

Take one glass before going to bed. Stay there for 48 hours, if you have no one to help you.

Traditionally, mathiglum was a mixture of honey and brandy. Brandy is made from distilled wine. Given the nature in which this mathiglum was made and administered, we are not sure of its applications. This recipe is included as a historical reference only.

Mrs. Weiler's Dropsy

2 qts hard cider
¼ lb juniper berries
¼ lb horseradish
¼ lb mustard seed
1/8 lb parsley root
1 gram of cream of tartar

Take a ½ wine glassful 3 times a day.

> Dropsy is an old medical term for edema, which is swelling of the tissues.
>
> Juniper berries and parsley root are said to have diuretic properties.

Mrs. Schooley's Dropsy

1 pint celery root
1 pint dandelion root
1 pint burdock root
1 gallon of water

Boil this down to 1 quart and strain. Take a tablespoon before a meal.

Herbal Remedies

> Dandelion and burdock contain diuretic properties which would help relieve edema. Celery is known for its capacity to lower blood pressure. Dandelion and celery are also rich in potassium which tend to be flushed from the body by diuretics, and therefore must be replaced to avoid potassium deficiency.

Clearfield

3 drams Sugar of lead
4 drams Sulfur
2 oz Bay Rum

2 oz Glycerin
1 ½ pt water

*Although this recipe does not include instructions with the list of ingredients, it was likely prepared as a medicinal lotion for several reasons. A **dram** is an apothecary unit of measure. Sugar of lead and sulfur are reported to have antibacterial and anti-parasitic properties. In addition, sugar of lead would dissolve in an alcohol, like the bay rum. Sugar of lead has been suggested for the historical treatment of poison ivy. It was also suggested for treatment of intestinal upsets.*

*Some historians propose that sugar of lead may have been the cause of Rome's downfall, since Romans would drink a sugar of lead syrup called **sapa** made from boiling grapes and water in lead drums. Lead poisoning causes lethargy and mental deteriorations, among other things. Today, use of this toxin is restricted mainly to dyes in hair coloring treatments. The recipe is included here as a historical reference.*

The "Run Around" meant that if an employee wasn't called in for work, then he/she could claim pay for the missed run.

Remover

One of the most satisfactory removers I have used may be made at home. It is comparatively inexpensive and does not injure wood. The remover I find most satisfactory is made of the following: one ounce ammonia, one ounce lye, and five ounces of water. Mix these thoroughly in a glass.

Apply this mixture on the surfaces from which paint is to be removed, let dry thoroughly, then rub off the paint with a clean piece of burlap. Should one application fail to remove all of the paint, apply another one.

Furniture Polish

1 gallon sweet oil
1 gallon kerosene
1 gallon rain water

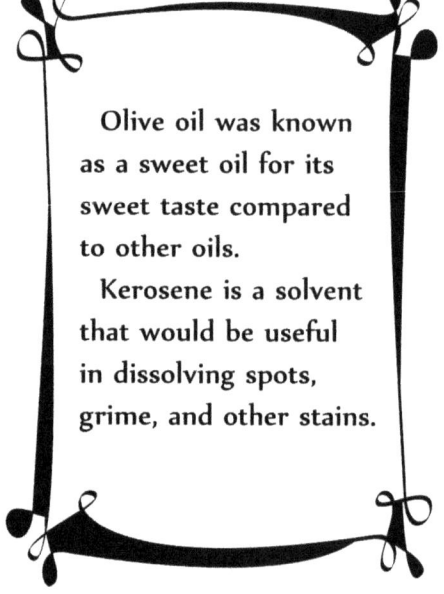

Olive oil was known as a sweet oil for its sweet taste compared to other oils.

Kerosene is a solvent that would be useful in dissolving spots, grime, and other stains.

ABOUT THE AUTHOR

Shaunda Kennedy Wenger is the great granddaughter of Elizabeth Shade Kennedy and an author of 8 books for children and co-author of a cookbook. *The Book Lover's Cookbook, Celebrated Works of Literature and the Passages That Feature Them* (Ballantine Books) was featured as a National Public Radio holiday gift pick in 2003. She has five titles published for the educational market, which include *Caterpillar Can't Wait, Watch a Butterfly Grow*, and *In Black Bear Country*. Her paranormal middle-grade novels, *The Ghost in Me* and *Reality Bites, Tales of a Half-Vampire*, have received much note-worthy praise. Her chapter book, *Little Red Riding Hood, Into the Forest Again*, won the 2011 KART Kids Book List Award for young readers and the 2012 Purple Dragonfly HM Award. For more information visit her blog at www.shaundawenger.blogspot.com.

Elizabeth Shade Kennedy with her son Harry
in 1903

www.ingramcontent.com/pod-product-compliance
Lightning Source LLC
Chambersburg PA
CBHW081326040426
42453CB00013B/2315